Milkvetch
&
Violets

Poems by
Mohammad Reza Shafi'i-Kadkani

EXPANDED BILINGUAL EDITION

Selected & Translated by
Mojdeh Bahar

MAGE PUBLISHERS

Mage Publishers Inc
www.mage.com

Library of Congress Cataloging-in-Publication Data
Available at the Library of Congress

Bilingual hardcover edition
ISBN 978-1-949445-75-6

English only paperback edition
ISBN 978-1-949445-32-9

Email: as@mage.com •
Mage online: www.mage.com

For Tina

Contents

Introduction

Mohammad Reza Shafi'i-Kadkani is a contemporary Iranian poet, literary critic, editor, author and translator. Born in 1939, his childhood days were divided between the village of Kadkan and the city of Mashhad in northeastern Iran. He was educated in the religious tradition for his primary and secondary education. He later earned his doctorate in Persian literature from Tehran University where he teaches today.

My introduction to Kadkani's poetry was at fourteen when I had left Iran for Europe and then the United States. I received a letter from my best friend who was still living in Iran. The letter contained the poem "Safe Travels!" which is included in this selection and has since become internationally known. It's also been put into songs by various vocalists. Milkvetch and breeze have a dialog in this poem, where the shackled plant asks that the free breeze carry a message to the blossoms and the rain, after traversing a tough terrain. The poem resonated deeply with me as its symbolism spoke to our predicament: one of us had left while the other had stayed put. For my family, like many others, leaving Iran represented freedom of thought and expression. It represented hope. In reading more of Kadkani's poetry I learned that in his nature poetry he acknowledges hardships but either anticipates and solves the problem, hopes for its future resolution or in the case of the inevitable, cautions the blossoms to prevent deception and loss. His wildflowers and birds anticipate the arrival of spring. His milkvetch contemplates its predicament but finds a way to convey its message through the breeze. His wintersweet outsmarts the drought; his mountain osier, pine and petunia are the songs of life; his rain cleanses the earth and purifies the words; his poppy is reckless, his sea fearless; his jasmines and sweetbriars are miraculous.

Persian poetry spans a millennium. Rudaki, a tenth century poet, is often considered the first Persian poet. From tenth to early twentieth century, namely 1920s, poets composed classical poems. Classical Persian poetry in its many forms and meters is highly structured and well defined. In 1920, Nima Yooshij, finding the classical structures restrictive, introduced *she'r-e no* "new poetry" and Nima became the father of modern Persian poetry. Since then, new poetry and classical poetry have coexisted. While some poets compose modern or classical poetry exclusively, others compose both classical and modern poetry. Mohammad Reza Shafi'i Kadkani is one such poet.

Kadkani wrote his first poem at the age of seven. In his three collections, spanning six decades, one can find traditional poetic forms such as *ghazal* (ode or sonnet) and *charpareh* (couplets) as well as Nimaic poems (free verse). Shafi'i Kadkani is at once a modern poet and a classical poet, well versed in both traditions. His themes, language, and style are unique, fusing the old with the new, the classic with the modern. His vocabulary is incredibly rich and deceptively simple. The beauty of his poetry resides in the union of these dualities. Literary critics describe his poetry as at times social and at other times naturalist. His poetry seems to occupy an in between space both in form and substance. He, unlike many of his contemporaries, is a harbinger of hope.

This selection is largely focused on Kadkani's poetry about nature that demonstrates both the dualities and the in between space of his writing. His seasons are not ordinary seasons, they are not easily defined, they capture the transitions between fall and winter, and the anticipation of spring. His highly musical verses emphasize movement and change in nature, and his nature is filled with possibilities and hope.

About this Edition

This is an expanded hardcover bilingual edition of a previously published English language only edition of the same name in 2021.

In addition to many scholarly books and articles, Mohammad Reza Shafi'i-Kadkani has published three volumes of poetry, each volume containing multiple previously published collections (he also writes under the pen name M. Sereshk*). The first volume *A Mirror for Voices* (1997) contains seven collections, the second volume *The Second Millennium of the Mountain Deer* (1999) and the third volume *A Child Named Joy* (2020) each contains five collections.

This selection includes sixty-one poems chosen from the three volumes. Fifty-six of the

---

* Pen names have long been used in Persian literature. They have been used as nouns, or subjects in a poem. They have also given poets an opportunity to comment on their own poetry or to use themselves as the interlocutor to indirectly convey a message to the reader. They can be chosen based on a variety of elements: the poet's birthplace, lineage, family traits, profession, as an homage to the poet's mentor, or as a shortened version of their name. Modern Persian poets have often chosen their pen names by using their first initial followed by a noun, for example: Mehdi Akhavan Sales's pen name is M. Omid; M (for his first initial) followed by Omid (hope); Ahmad Shamlou's pen name is A. Bamdad (morning); and Mohammad Reza Shafi'i Kadkani's pen name is M. Sereshk (tear, and also dew or rain). Interestingly, this nomenclature is limited to men. Although at times contemporary women poets have used a pseudonym in some of their poems, e.g. Simin Behbahani signs some of her poems as Kowli (Gypsy).

poems explore themes through nature or natural elements generally; and plants, seasons, storms, and different forms of water specifically. Five of the poems, "Compass," "Missing," "Clock and Calendar," and "Poetry Therapy," and "Windlass," though not related to nature, are too beautiful to leave out.

The poet has dated and indicated the location for only some of the poems. The dates are sometimes specific, and at other times only a month, year or a season is mentioned.

Poems

کوهبید

در آغوشِ این درّهٔ دیر سال
بر این صخرهٔ خامشِ کور و کر
درختِ تک افتادهٔ کوهبید
برآورده، مغرور، بر ابر، سر.
فروبرده در سینهٔ تنگِ سنگ
پیِ جستنِ زندگی ریشه‌ها
نه از تیشهٔ تیزِ برقش هراس
نه از خشمِ طوفانش اندیشه‌ها
در آنجا که ابری نباریده است
در آنجا که نگذشته یک رهگذار
درختِ تک افتادهٔ کوهبید
سرودِ حیات است سبز و بلند
شکفته چنین بر لبِ کوه سار

کدکن، مرداد ۱۳٤۳

Mountain Osier*

Embraced by this ancient valley
On this silent, blind and deaf rock
The lonesome mountain osier
   peers proudly over the clouds.

Piercing the narrow bosom of the rock
With its roots searching for life
No fear of the sharp hatchet of lightning
Nor thoughts of the raging storm.

Where no cloud has caused rain
Where no passerby has passed
The lonesome mountain osier
   is the song of life, green and tall
   budding at the edge of the cliff.

Jul/Aug 1964
Kadkan

---

* [Poet's footnote]: Mountain Osier (Willow) is a wild willow, with narrow leaves, it is drought tolerant and grows in dry valleys or amid rocks.

زنهار

ای شاخهٔ شکوفهٔ بادام!
خوب آمدی-
سلام!
لبخند می زنی؟
امّا
این باغ بی نجابت
با این شبِ ملول...
زنهار از این نسیمَکِ آرام!
وین گاه گه نوازشِ ایام!
بیهوده خنده می زنی افسوس!
بِفشار در رکابِ خموشی
پای درنگ را.
باور مکن که ابر...
باور مکن که باد...
باور مکن که خندهٔ خورشیدِ بامداد...
من می شناسم این همه نیرنگ و رنگ را

مشهد، اسفند ۱۳٤۳

Beware...

O branch of almond blossom!
Welcome–
Greetings!

You're smiling?
But
This indecent grove
   with this lonesome night...
Beware of this faint little breeze!
   this intermittent caress of time!

You laugh in vain, alas!
Press the foot of delay
   in the stirrup of silence.

Don't believe the cloud...
Don't believe the wind...
Don't believe the laughter of the morning sun...
I only know all these dyes and deceptions.

Feb/Mar 1965
Mashhad

5

باغِ خودرو

خروسِ خانهٔ همسایه می خوانْد
و بارانِ سحرگاهانِ اسفند
فرو می ریخت از ابری شتابان.

گریزان ابرها، بر آبیِ صبح
ـ چنان چون قاصدک بر کاسنی زار ـ
روان بودند زی کوه و بیابان.

و من در اوجِ آن لحظه یْ خدایی
در آن اندیشهَ و آن بیشه بودم
که در آن سوی باغ پر گلِ ابر
دران ژرفِ کبود آیا کسی هست
که این باغ شفق گلخانهٔ اوست
و فانوسِ بلورینِ ستاره
ـ بر این نیلی رواقِ جاودان دور ـ
چراغِ روشنِ کاشانهٔ اوست،
و یا این باغْ،
خودروی ست و خود روست؟

مشهد، بهار ۱۳۴۲

6

Wild Garden

The neighbor's rooster was crowing,
The raindrops of a March dawn
   falling from a hurried cloud.

The fleeting clouds, in the blue morning sky
—like a blowball* on a chicory field—
   flowing from the mountain and the desert.

And I, at the height of that Godly moment,
Deep in thought in the woods,
   whether on the other side of this garden of
   cloud flowers
   in that deep azure, there is someone
   for whom this garden is a greenhouse
   and the crystalline lantern of the star
   —in this enduring, vast royal blue sky—
   serves as the bright light of his house,
Or whether this garden,
   is wild, crawling and self-sustaining?

Spring 1963
Mashhad

---

* The fluffy seed ball of a dandelion. Also referred to as
dandelion clock.

7

کدامین انتظاری

بخوان ای چرخ ریسَک! نغمه ات را
– بران شاخ برهنه یْ بی گل و برگ –
که داری انتظارِ نو بهاری.

ولی من، این دلِ بی آرزو را
–که از شور قیامت هم نجنبد–
کنم خوش با کدامین انتظاری؟

مشهد، بهمن ۱۳٤۲

Which Anticipation...?

Sing, O titmouse, your song!
   —on that bare, flowerless, leafless branch—
   for you anticipate the arrival of spring.

But, with which anticipation shall I delight
   this despairing heart of mine
   —that's not fazed by a thing?

Jan/Feb 1964
Mashhad

سفر به خیر

- « به کجا چنین شتابان؟ »
گَوَن از نسیم پرسید.

- « دلِ من گرفته زینجا،
هوسِ سفر نداری
ز غبار این بیابان؟ »

- « همه آرزویم، امّا
چه کنم که بسته پایم... »

- « به کجا چنین شتابان؟ »

- « به هر آن کجا که باشد به جز این سرا، سرایم. »

- « سفرت به خیر! امّا، تو و دوستی، خدا را
چو از این کویرِ وحشت به سلامتی گذشتی،
به شکوفه‌ها، به باران،
برسان سلامِ ما را. »

Safe Travels!

"Where to, in such a rush?"
  the milkvetch* asked the breeze.

"I feel depressed here.
Don't you have the desire
  to leave this dusty desert?"

"I am all desire
Alas,
I am shackled here."

"Where to, in such a rush?"

"Anywhere, but here,
where I can feel at home."

"Safe travels
But
For us and for God,
Once you have traversed this desert of dread,
Convey our regards!†
To the blossoms, to the rain"

---

* Many species of milkvetch grow in Iran, more than
half of which are native plants. They are bushes with
beautifully colored flowers. They grow in many parts of
the country including the province of Khorasan, where
the poet was born. In North America, some species of
milkvetch are known as locoweed.

† In 2015 this poem was inscribed on a wall in
Clarensteeg in Leiden, Netherlands with an English
translation by Dick Davis entitled "Travel Safely!"

پرسش

گیرم که این درختِ تناور
در قلّهٔ بلوغ
آبستن از نسیمِ گناهی ست؛

امّا
-ای ابر سوگوارِ سیه پوش!-
این شاخهٔ شکوفه چه کرده ست
کاین سان کبود مانده و خاموش ؟

گیرم خدا نخواست که این باغِ
بیند ز ابر و باد نوازش
امّا
این شاخهٔ شکوفه که افسرد
– از سردی بهار
با گونهٔ کبود –
آیا چه کرده بود؟

مشهد، اسفند ۱۳٤۳

12

Query

Suppose that this robust tree
  at the peak of maturity
  is impregnated by a sinful breeze;

But
—O grieving black cloaked cloud!—
What have these blossoms done
  to be left bruised and silent?

Suppose God did not want this garden
  to be caressed by the cloud or the wind,
This branch with blossoms, wilted by the cold
  spring,
Turned blue,
What had it done?

Feb/Mar 1965
Mashhad

سفرنامهٔ باران

آخرین برگِ سفرنامهٔ باران،
این است:
که زمین چرکین است.

Rain's Travelogue

The last page of rain's travelogue reads:
The earth is filthy.

ترديد

گفتم : « - بهار آمده. » گفتی :
« - امّا درخت ها را
اندیشهٔ بلندِ شکفتن نیست.
گویا درخت ها
باور نمی کنند که این ابر،
این نسیم
پیغام آن حقیقتِ سبز است. »

« - آری بهار جامهٔ سبزی نیست
تا هر کسی
هر لحظه ای که خواست
به دوشش بیفکند. »

تهران، اسفند ۱۳٤٥

16

Doubt

I said: "Spring has arrived."
You said: "Yet trees have no aspiration of
  blooming.
As if the trees
  don't believe that this cloud,
  this breeze
  are the harbingers of that green truth."

"Indeed, spring is not a green robe
  that one can wear
  upon desire."

February 1967
Tehran

17

کوچِ بنفشه‌ها

در روزهای آخر اسفند
کوچِ بنفشه‌های مهاجر،
زیباست.

در نیمِ روزِ روشنِ اسفند،
وقتی بنفشه‌ها را از سایه‌های سرد،
در اطلسِ شمیمِ بهاران،
با خاک و ریشه
– میهنِ سیّارشان –
در جعبه‌های کوچکِ چوبی
در گوشهٔ خیابان می‌آورند:

جوی هزار زمزمه در من،
می‌جوشد:
ای کاش...
ای کاش آدمی وطنش را
مثلِ بنفشه‌ها
(در جعبه‌های خاک)
یک روز می‌توانست،
همراهِ خویشتن ببرد هرکجا که خواست.
در روشنای باران،
در آفتابِ پاک.

اسفند ۱۳٤۵

18

Migration of Violets

In late winter,
  the migration of nomadic violets
  is beautiful.

In the midday light, in March,
When enveloped in spring scented satin,
With root and soil
  —their portable home—
In small wooden boxes
Out of the cold shadows
  to street corners they are transported:

A stream of thousand chants resonate inside
  of me:
I wish...
I wish, like violets (in soil–filled boxes),
  one day, one could
  take one's homeland along to wherever
  one desired.
In light of rain
In pure sunlight.

Feb/Mar 1967

در حضورِ باد

کلماتم را
در جوی سحر می شویم
لحظه هایم را
در روشنیِ باران ها
تا برای تو شعری بسرایم روشن.
تا که بی دغدغه
بی ابهام
سخنانم را
درحضورِ باد
– این سالکِ دشت وهامون –
با تو بی پرده بگویم
که تو را
دوست می دارم تا مرزِ جنون

مرداد ۱۳٤٦

In the Presence of the Wind

My words
I wash them in the stream of dawn;
My moments,
In the light of rain;
So I can write you an honest poem
So with no concern
No ambiguity,
And the wind as my witness,
My words
   —those of a nomad of plains & deserts—
   will assure you:
I love you to the brink of madness!

Jul/Aug 1967

پاسخ

هیچ میدانی چرا، چون موج،
در گریز ازخویشتن، پیوسته می کاهم؟
زان که بر این پردهٔ تاریک،
این خاموشیِ نزدیک،
آنچه می خواهم نمی بینم،
وآنچه می بینم نمی خواهم.

تهران، یازدهم مرداد ۱۳٤٦

Response

Do you know why, like the wave,
   as I redound, I am steadily reduced?
For on this opaque veil,
In this inner darkness,
What I want, I don't see,
&
What I see, I don't want.

Aug 2, 1967
Tehran

23

ملال

در کنارِ جوی
من نشسته،
آب در رفتار.

در تمامِ هفته،
خسته،
انتظارِ جمعه را دارم
در تمامِ جمعه
باز از فرطِ تنهایی
انتظارِ شنبه است و کار...

من نشسته
آب در رفتار.

آذر ۱۳٤٦

Languor

On a stream bank
I sit
Water flows.

All week,
Tired
I anticipate Friday.*
All day Friday
   in utter loneliness
   yet again
I anticipate Saturday and work...

I sit
Water flows.

Nov/Dec 1967

---

* In Iran, the work week is from Saturday to Thursday
and Friday is a day of rest.

دریا

حسرت نبرم به خوابِ آن مرداب
کآرام درونِ دشتِ شب خفته ست.
دریایم و نیست باکم از طوفان:
دریا، همه عمر، خوابش آشفته ست.

تهران ۱۳٤٦

Sea

I don't envy the swamp's slumber
Asleep in the dead of night peacefully.
I am the sea, fearless of the storm:
The sea, forever sleeping fitfully.

1967
Tehran

آبی

لحظهٔ خوب
لحظهٔ ناب.

لحظهٔ آبیِ صبحِ اسفند
لحظهٔ ابرهای شناور
لحظه ای روشن و
ژرف و جاری
ـ حاصلِ معنیِ جملهٔ آب.

لحظه ای که در آن خنده هایت
جذبه را تا صنوبر رسانید
لحظهٔ آبیِ باغِ بیدار
لحظهٔ روشن و نغزِ دیدار.

تهران، ۱۴ تیر ماه ۱۳۴۷

Clear Blue

The fine moment
The pure moment.

The clear blue moment of a March morning,
The moment of floating clouds,
A moment, bright and
    deep & flowing
    —the very essence of water.

A moment when your laughter
    delivered rapture to the fir,
The clear blue moment of the awakened
    garden,
The bright moment and the rare reunion.

July 5, 1968
Tehran

سیاه قلم

دستِ خشکِ زمستان ازین باغ
رنگ ها را بدان سان ربوده ست
کز شگفتی تو گویی، در اینجا،
هیچ باغ و بهاری نبوده ست.

تهران ۱۳٤۸

Pen and Ink

The dry hand of winter
  has stripped the garden of color
Astonished, you presume,
There has never been a garden nor a
  spring here.

1969
Tehran

نمازی در تنگنا

زان سویِ بهار و زان سویِ باران
زان سویِ درخت و
زان سویِ جوبار
در دور ترین فواصلِ هستی
نزدیک ترین مخاطبِ من باش

نه بانگِ خروس است و
نه مهتاب
نه دمدمهٔ سپیده دم، امّا
تو آینه دارِ روشناییِ صبح
در خلوتِ خالیِ شبِ من باش!

تهران، ۲۸ دی ماه ۱۳٤۸

A Prayer in Strait

From beyond spring and rain
From beyond tree and stream
From the farthest corners of the universe
Be my closest confidant!

There's no rooster's crow
No moonlight
No break of dawn.
Be the dawn of day
   in the lonely solitude of my night!

Jan 18,1970
Tehran

33

جوانی

این گلِ سرخ
این گلِ سرخ صد برگِ شاداب
این گلِ سرخَ تاج خدایان
که به هر روزَ برگی از آن را
می کَنی با سرانگشتِ نفرت

– تا نبینی که پژمردگی هاش
می شود درنظر ها نمایان –
چند روزِ دگر برگ هایش
می رسد، اندک اندک، به پایان.

تهران، ۲۳ بهمن ۱۳۴۸

34

Youth

This red rose
This fresh red rose of a hundred petals
This red rose of the Gods' crowns
   whose petals you pluck everyday with
   hatred
   one by one
   —so not to witness others perceive its
   wilting—
In a few days its petals,
Will gradually disappear.

Feb 12, 1970
Tehran

زندگی نامهٔ شقایق ۱

زندگی نامهٔ شقایق چیست؟

– رایتِ خون به دوش، وقتِ سحر،

نغمه ای عاشقانه بر لبِ باد؛

زندگی را سپرده در رهِ عشق،

به کفِ باد و هرچه باداباد.

تهران ۱۳۵۰

Poppy's Life Story 1

What is the poppy's life story?

Shouldering a banner of blood at dawn,
The wind and its romantic aria,
Entrusting its life on the path of love,
  to the wind and que sera, sera.*

1971/72
Tehran

---

* While the correct expression *quel che sarà sarà* is Italian.
A song, popularized in the 1950s by Doris Day, spelled
the expression que sera, sera as if it were Spanish. This
expression is now part of the English language, and many
others.

در اقلیم پاییز

آن بلوطِ کهن، آنجا، بنگر
نیم پاییزی و نیمیش بهار:
مثلِ این است که جادوی خزان
تا کمرگاهش،
با زحمت،
رفته ست و از آنجا دیگر
نتوانسته بالا برود.

اکسفورد، پاییز ۱۹۷٤

Autumnal Climate

Behold the old chestnut tree, over there,
Half autumnal, half vernal:
As if the magic of fall
   has laboriously climbed up to its waist
And from there,
   could go no further.

Fall 1974
Tehran

زندگی نامهٔ شقایق ۲

آه ای شقایقانِ بهارانِ من!
یاران من!
از خاک و خاره، خونِ شما را
حتّی
طوفانِ نوح نیز نیارد سترد،
زانک
هر لحظه گسترانگی اش بیش می شود؛
آن گونه ای که باران،
هر چند تندتر
رخسارِ ارغوان
شاداب و
سرخ گونه تر از پیش می شود.

اکسفورد، ژانویه ۱۹۷۵

Poppy's Life Story 2

O poppies of my springs!
My darlings!
Your blood shall not be expunged,
  from soil or stone,
Not even by Noah's flood
For it spreads forever more
The same way the rain,
  ever more rapidly
  renders the face of the Judas tree,
  lush and more rosy-cheeked than before.

Jan. 1975
Oxford

41

مزمورِ درخت

ترجیح می دهم که درختی باشم
در زیر تازیانهٔ کولاک و آذرخش
با پویهٔ شکفتن و گفتن
تا
رامْ صخره ای
در ناز و در نوازشِ باران
خاموش از برای شنفتن.

اکسفورد، دسامبر ۱۹۷۵

Tree's Psalm

I'd rather be a tree
   flogged by blizzard and thunder
   dynamically burgeoning and booming
Than a meek rock
   cuddled and caressed by rain
   silently listening.

Dec. 1975
Oxford

مناجات

فاصرفِ الخاطرَ عن ظاهرِها

ابن عربی

می شناسمت

چشم های تو

میزبانِ آفتابِ صبحِ سبزِ باغ‌هاست.

می شناسمت

واژه های تو،

کلیدِ قفل های ماست.

می شناسمت

آفریدگار و یارِ روشنی

دست های تو

پلی به رؤیتِ خداست.

پرینستون، ۱٦ دسامبر ۱۹۷۵

44

Hymn

So dismiss the appearance from your mind

Ibn Arabi[*]

I know you
Your eyes
The hosts of sunlight in spring dawn in the
    gardens.

I know you
Your words
The keys to our locks.

I know you
Creator and companion of light,
Your hands
A bridge to seeing God.

Dec. 16, 1975
Princeton

---

[*] Ibn Arabi is a Sufi mystic saint and poet. In the next
phrase—which Kadkani has not included—Ibn Arabi
continues, "and seek the essence to get to know it". One
could simplify the quote to "forget the appearance, seek
the essence, in order to know it."

در سوگِ آن عُصاره‌ٔ طوفان

از تارهای صوتیِ باران
بشنو، درین غروبِ بهاران
این شعر نیست، پردهٔ خون است
ویرانیِ من است و شمایان
عصیان معنی است بر الفاظ،
در نایِ آذرخشِ خروشان
دندانْ غروچهٔ کلمات است
در سوگِ آن عصارهٔ طوفان.

۱۳۵٤

Mourning the Essence of the Storm

Listen to the vocal cords of rain,
   in this sunset of springs!

This is not a poem, it's a curtain of blood
It's my destruction and yours.

It's the mutiny of meaning against sound,
   in the trachea of roaring thunder.

Words grinding their teeth
Mourning the essence of the storm.

1975/76

ژانویه

با چنین قامت بالندهٔ سبز
کاج،
در باغ،
خدایی ابدی ست
گوشِ سرشارِ نمازِ باران.

بهرِ میلادِ پسر خواندهٔ خاک
مشکنیدش مبریدش یاران!

تهران، ژانویه ۱۹۷۶

January

The pine's glorious green stature
   in the grove
   is an eternal God
   with an earful of rain's prayers.

Companions, in honor of the birth of soil's
   stepson
Do not break it, do not cut it down!

Jan. 1976
Tehran

49

به برگِ گلِ سرخ

بدان سان که باران
سوی آسمان راه برگشت هرگز ندارد
من این راه را تا به پایانِ پاییز
به پایِ پر از زخم، خواهم سپردن.

به آب و به آیینه، سوگند، یاران!
من این حزن را از رخِ کودکانِ نشابور
به برگِ گلِ سرخ خواهم ستردن.

پرینستون، ۱۹۷٦

50

With the Rose Petal

As raindrops
  never return to the sky,
with wounded feet
I will stay the course to the end of Fall.

Friends!
I vow to water,
I vow to mirror,
  to wipe the sorrow off the faces of the
  children of Neyshabur*
  with a rose petal.

1976
Princeton

---

* A city in Khorasan in northeastern Iran,
75 kilometers from the poet's birthplace, Kadkan.

سبزیِ خزه

شوخْ چشمیِ خزه
رودخانه را فریب می دهد که می رَوَم
ولی نمی رود
سال ها و سال هاست.
رودخانه بارها
رنگِ خون گرفته در سپیده دم
سبزیِ خزه
همچنان بر آب ها رهاست
می نماید این که می روم ، ولی نمی رود
همچنان به جاست.

رودخانه صخره را ربود و برد
لیک سبزیِ خزه
می نماید این که می روم ، ولی نمی رود
ایستاده مثلِ اژدهاست.

رودخانه را فریب می دهد
سال ها و سال ها و سال هاست.

اکسفورد، ۱۷ آوریل ۱۹۷٦

The Greenness of Moss

The impudence of moss
   tricks the river that it is leaving
Yet it stays put
It's been years and years.

Many a time the river
   crimson at dawn
The greenness of moss
Still floating in the water
Pretends to leave
Yet it stays put.
It still remains.

The river ran off with the rock
But the greenness of moss
Pretends to leave, yet it stays put
Standing like a dragon.

It tricks the river
It's been years and years and years.

April 17, 1976
Oxford

حَسبِ حال

شب آمد و گِردِ روز پرگار گرفت،
بر صبح و سپیده راهِ دیدار گرفت،
چندان که درونِ سینه و دفتر ماند،
آواز و سرود و شعر زنگار گرفت.

Current Mood

Night fell and enveloped the day,
For dawn and morning it blocked the way

Too long in the bosom and notebook it
   remained,
Song, lyrics and poem all decayed.

در برابرِ درخت

صبحِ زود بود،
باغ، پُر صنوبر و
سرود بود.

سینه سرخ ها در اوج ها و
اوج ها،
پر گشوده فوج ها و
فوج ها،
می زد از کرانِ شرق،
در نگاهشان
شعاعِ شیریِ سحر،
موجَ ها و مَوج ها و موج ها.
هر گیاه وبرگُچچه در آستانهٔ سحر،
آن صدای سبز را،
- زان سوی جدارِ حرف و
صوت -
می چشید.
آن صدا که موسی از درخت می شنید.

گر چه خویش را
ز خویشتن
تکانده بودم و رها شده،
باز هم در آن میان غریبه بودم و کسی،
از حضورِ من خبر نداشت.

هرچه واژه داشتم نثار کردم و درخت،
لحظه ای مرا به کُنهِ خویش ره نداد.

Before the Tree

Early morning,
The garden brimming with spruce firs
and songs.

Robins soaring
& soaring
Wings spread, in droves &
droves
From the eastern horizon
The milky ray of dawn
reflected in their gaze,
in waves & waves & waves.

At twilight, every plant & leaflet
would taste
that green sound,
—from the other side of the wall separating
speech & sound—
The sound that Moses would hear from the
tree.

Though I was rid of my self
and set free
There, I remained a stranger & no one
was aware of my presence.

I offered all my words
Yet the tree
did not let me in, not even for a moment.

ناکجا

من و شعر و جویبار
رفتیم و
رفتیم،
به آنجا رسیدیم آنجا که دیگر،
نه جا پای کس بود و
نه آشنا بود.

درختان به آیین دیگر،
و مرغان به آیین دیگر،
صدایی که می آمد از دور،
صدای خدا بود،
رها بود.

به هنگامِ پرواز
از روی باغی به باغی،
کسی زیرِ بالِ پرستو و
پروانه ها را،
نمی کرد تفتیش،
شقایق،
ز طوفان نمی گشت خاموش،
چراغش همیشه پر از روشنا بود.

نمی دانم آنجا کجا بود،
نمی دانم آنجا کجا بود.

No Man's Land

I, along with the poem and the stream,
We went
And went,
We reached a place where
   there were no footsteps,
Nothing familiar.

Where trees were of a different kind,
Birds of a different flock.
A voice from afar,
The voice of God,
Free.

While flying,
   from one garden to another
Nobody would inspect
   the underwings of swallows,
   of butterflies,
The poppy
   would not be silenced by the storm
Its light always brightly shone.

I do not know where that was!
I do not know where that was!

پرسش ۲

این نه اگر معجزه ست پاسختان چیست؟
در نَفَسِ اژدها چگونه شکفته ست
این همه یاسِ سپید و نسترنِ سرخ؟

Inquiry 2

If not by a miracle
How do you explain
   blooming in the dragon's breath
   countless white jasmines and red sweetbriers?

آوازه پرنده

برسرِ ساقهٔ سبزِ شمشاد
مرغکی شاد
آوازخوان است.
— کس چه داند که رازی نهانی ست —
شاید آوازخوان شد ز شادی
یا که شادیش ز آوازخوانی ست.

Birdsong

On a green boxwood branch
   a joyful little bird sings
– Nobody knows for it's
   a well-kept secret –
Maybe it sings out of joy
Maybe it's joyful because it sings!

آرایشِ خورشید

اگر می شد صدا را دید
چه گل هایی!
چه گل هایی!
که از باغِ صدای تو
به هر آواز می شد چید.

اگر می شد صدا را دید.... .

۲۳ مرداد ۱۳۶٦

Sun's Makeup

If sound were visible
What flowers
        What flowers
Could be picked from the garden of your
    voice
    with each song!

If only sound were visible...

August 14, 1987

برگِ درختان سبز

...هر ورقش دفتری است
سعدی

نسیمی ورق می زند
برگ های سپیدار را
در شعاعِ گلِ زرد
و گنجشکَ، با هوشیاری،
می آموزد از هر ورق گونه گون معرفت ها:

که این باغ در هسته ای بوده
وان هسته درهسته ای
تا جهان بوده این هسته
پیوسته بوده ست.

نسیمی وَرَق می زند برگ های سپیدار را
در شعاعِ گلِ زرد
و گنجشکَ با هوشیاری
می آموزد از هر ورق گونه گون معرفت ها:
که گنجشک از بیضه و بیضه از ذاتِ گنجشک
و گنجشک در ذاتِ بیضه ست.

66

Leaf of Green Trees

"Every one of its leaves is a notebook"[*]
Sa'adi

The breeze leafs through
  the leaves of the white poplar
  in the radius of the yellow flower
And the sparrow, cleverly,
  learns from each leaf a different lesson:

That this garden used to be in a seed
And that seed in yet another seed
As long as the world has existed,
  this seed too has existed.

The breeze leafs through
  the leaves of the white poplar
  in the radius of the yellow flower
And the sparrow, cleverly,
  learns from each leaf a different lesson:
That the sparrow comes from an egg,
And that egg from the essence of the sparrow
And the sparrow is from the heart of the egg.

---

[*] The poem refers to a verse of a poem by Sa'adi, a
thirteenth century Iranian poet. It can be translated as:
   The green leaves of trees before God,
   each leaf is a notebook with lessons by the creator

نسیمی ورق می زند برگ های سپیدار را:
که دریاست زین رود و این رود
از قطرهٔ ابر و ابر
از زه و زادِ دریاست.

نسیمی نمی آید و برگ های سپیدار
از جنبشِ خویش باز ایستاده ست
و گنجشك زآموزشِ معرفت بازمانده ست،
و بسیارها پرسش از خاطرِ او
گذر دارد و هیچ پاسخ ندارد
که دیگر کتابی نخوانده ست.

۱۳٦۷

The breeze leafs through
   the leaves of the white poplar:
That the sea is from this river
   and this river from rain clouds
And the clouds are the progeny of the sea.

There is no breeze and the leaves of the
   white poplar
   no longer move
And the sparrow no longer learns any
   lessons,
Many questions occupy its mind
Remain unanswered
For it has not read any more books.

1988/89

برگِ بی درخت

در قرائتِ پُل سلان

گر درختی از خزان بی برگ شد
یا کرخت ازسورتِ سرمای سخت
هست امّیدی که ابرِ فرودین
برگها رویانَدَش از فرِّ بخت.
بر درختِ زنده بی برگی چه غم؟
وای بر احوالِ برگِ بی درخت!

۱۲ شهریور ۱۳۶۶

A Treeless Leaf

*In reading Paul Celan**

If a tree becomes leafless in the fall,
Or numb due to the bitter cold
There is hope that the spring cloud
   will sprout its leaves as it brings relief.
The tree can live leafless
What's the grief?
Lament the condition of the treeless leaf!

Sept. 3, 1987

---

* Paul Celan is a Jewish Romanian-born poet, polyglot, translator and lecturer who wrote poems in Romanian and German. He was born in 1920 and drowned himself in the Seine in 1970. His life during the Holocaust was a major influence in his literary work. Survival (of a person as well as a language) and the importance of language are among the themes explored by Celan.

تحمّلِ خار

آمد بهار و برگی و باری نداشتم
چون شاخهٔ بریدهٔ بهاری نداشتم

دراین چمن چو آتشِ سردی که لاله داشت
می سوختم نهان و شراری نداشتم

گل خنده زد به شاخ و من ازخویش شرمسار
کاندر بهاربرگی و باری نداشتم

دادم ز دست دامنت ای گل به طعنه ای
از باغِ تو تحمّلِ خاری نداشتم

یك دم به آستانِ تو بختم نبُرد راه
در کویت اعتبارغباری نداشتم.

Withstanding a Thorn

Spring arrived and a leaf or fruit I had not
Like a cut branch, spring I had not

In this field, like tulip's center burnt to a coal,
I burned in secret and a spark I had not

The flower smiled at the branch and I ashamed
  of myself
For at springtime a leaf or fruit I had not

Flower! I lost you to a single taunt
The strength to withstand a thorn from your
  garden I had not

Not for a moment did my fortune lead me to
  your doorstep
For you, the value of a speck of dust, I had not.

سفر در برگِ نیلوفر

آسمان بسیار است
آسمان هاست به رنگِ شنگرف
آسمان هاست به رنگِ زیتون
آسمان هاست ز فیروزهٔ نیشابوری
که مرا در آن سیر و سفری ست.

آسمانِ سَحَری در پی باران بهار
آسمانِ خزر آمیخته با تودهٔ ابر و زنگار
لحظه هایی که در آن پرتوِ صبح و سَحَری ست.

لیک در قطرهٔ باران
که برین نیلوفر
ـ غم و شادی به هم آمیخته
چون رنج وهنر ـ
راستی باید گفت :
آسمانِ دگری است!

۱۳۶۸

۷۴

A Journey in the Lily Pad

There are many skies
Skies the color of astonishment
Skies the color of olive
Skies the color of Neyshaburi turquoise
I travel through them all.

Dawn sky after spring showers,
Caspian sky mixed with clouds and
    verdigris
Moments of morning rays and daybreak.

Yet in the raindrop
On this lily
—Sorrow and joy interwoven
Like suffering and art—
One should note:
It's a different sky!

1989/90

گلِ آفتابگردان

گل آفتابگردان و
نمازِ آفتابش
به شب و
به ابر و
ظلمت
نشود دَمی بر او گُم
دلِ اوست قبله یابش!

Sunflower

Sunflower
And its prayer to the Sun
      At night
            With clouds
                  In the dark
Not for a moment loses
  its solar compass,
  stowed deep within its soul!

❋

گل‌های نقشِ کاشی

گنجشک، در تمامِ زمستان،
ز اشتیاق
از بس که بهرِ باغ و بهار انتظار دید
گل‌های نقشِ کاشیِ مسجد را
در نیمه‌های دی
صبحِ بهار دید.

Floral Tile Design

The sparrow, throughout winter
        Longing
with such anticipation of garden and spring
    that she perceived the floral tile in the
    mosque,
        in January,
    as the dawn of spring

قطب‌نما

نه رهنما و نه رهنامه و نه ره پیداست.

دوگام سوی شمال و دو گام سوی جنوب
مسافری که تویی در شعاعِ این ظلمت،
نگاه می کنی و فرصتت هُبوب و هباست.

سزای همچو تویی چیست غیرِ در ماندن
به هر که بود و به هرجا که بود و هرچه که بود
رجوع کردی، اِلّا دلت که قطب نماست.

۲۲ فروردین ۱۳۷۲

Compass

No guide, no map, no clear path

Two steps north
Two steps south
You who travels through this darkness
You blink and your opportunity is but ruin
  and collapse.

What do you deserve if not destitute?
For you sought everyone, everything,
  everywhere, but your own heart,
  your compass.

April 19, 1993

پنجه در پنجهٔ مرگ

باد را بین که پیچیده، بیرحم،
تا جدا سازد این شاخه از برگ
برگ را بین که با عشقِ سبزش
می زَنَد پنجه در پنجهٔ مرگ.

۹ اریبهشت ۱۳۷۲

Claw to Claw with Death

Look at the cruel wind twist,
  to separate this branch from the leaf
Look at the leaf with its green love
  fight claw to claw with death.

April 29, 1993

قاصدک ها

باد
کژ مژ
می وَزَد
اینجا
و مجموعی
گلِ قاصد
می رسند از هر طرف
چندان
کزانبوهی
می دهند آزارِ چشم وسَدِّ دیدارند.

من یقین دارم خبرهاشان دروغین است
قاصدك ها بس که بسیارند.

۲۵ اردیبهشت ۱۳۷۸

Blowballs

Wind
  Crookedly
    Blows
      Here
      And a bunch of
         blowballs
            Blow in from all sides
 and
   their bushiness
bothers the eye and blocks the vision.

I am certain they bear false news
As there is a bounty of blowballs!

May 15, 1993

از اورادِ گُلِ سرخ

بعد از دی دیوانه وآن سردی دیرَنْد
وان پیرْیخِ نیمهٔ دی ماه شکستن،
بسیار نپایَد
این لحظهٔ سرمای گُلِ سرخ
این لحظهٔ خون خوردن وخاموش نشستن.

فروردین ۱۳۵۸

Cold Snap

After the long winter
  and
  the bitter cold
  cracking the mid-winter firn,*
This dogwood winter†
This suffering and silence
Will not endure.

March 2006

❄

---

* Firn is the intermediate stage between snow and ice.

† Dogwood winters are cold spells or short winter-
like periods after the arrival of spring.

موعظهٔ غوك

در هجومِ تشنگی، درسوزِ خورشیدِ تموز
پای در زنجیرِ خاکِ تفته می‌نالَد گَوَن:
«روزها را می‌کنم، پیمانه، با آمد شدن.»

غوکِ نیزارانِ لای و لوش گوید در جواب:
«چند وچند این تشنگی؟ خود را رها کن همچو ما
پیش نِه گامی و جامی نوش و کوته کن سخن.»

بوتهٔ خشکِ گَوَن درپاسخش گوید: «خَمُش!
پایْ درزنجیر، خوش‌تر، تا که دست اندر لجن.»

۱۰ آوریل ۱۹۷۶

88

Toad's Admonition

Under thirst's attack in the blazing July sun
Shackled in scorching soil
The milkvetch laments:
"I spend my days noting the passage of time"

The toad in a cane thicket of slime and sludge
  responds:
"How long will you endure this thirst?
Liberate yourself like us,
Step forward, take a sip, shorten the rhyme"

The dry milkvetch bush says in response:
  "Hush!
Feet in shackles are more honorable than
  hands in slime"

April 10, 1976

شعر درمانی

هر دم به اشارات، شدم هر سویی
شاید که بیابم از شفایی، بویی
دردا که نیافتم به قانون، جز شعر،
از بهر نجاتِ روحِ خود دارویی

Poetry Therapy

Every moment, with the slightest hint,*
  I went in every direction
  to find the possible hint of a cure
Alas, in *The Canon*,† I found no potion
  but poetry
  to salvage my soul.

---

* In the Persian text the word *isharat* ("hints")
is used, which could indicate a reference
to one of Avicenna's philosophical works,
namely *Al-Isharat wa al-Tanbinat* (Remarks and
Admonitions).

† *The Canon of Medicine* is a medical
encyclopedia by Avicenna, a 10–11th century
philosopher and physician.

گمشده

طفلی به نامِ شادی، دیری است گم شده ست
با چشم های روشنِ برّاق
با گیسویی بلند، به بالای آرزو.

هر کس ازو نشانی دارد،
ما را کند خبر
این هم نشان ما:
یک سو خلیج فارس
سویِ دگر خزر

Missing

A child named Joy has long been missing
With bright light eyes
With hair as long as hope.

If you know of her whereabouts,
Contact us.
Here's our address:
At one end, Persian Gulf
At the other, Caspian Sea.

❖

به دنبالِ آن لحظهٔ جاودانی

ورق می زنم برگ های گل اطلسی را
ورق می زنم
سالها
روزها را
ورق می زنم آسمان را
زمین را
ورق می زنم
عمر را
آشکارونهانی
به دنبالِ آن لحظهٔ جاودانی.

In Search of that Everlasting Moment

I leaf through petunia petals
I leaf through
  the years
  the days
I leaf through the sky
  the earth
I leaf through life
  openly and secretly
  in search of that everlasting moment.

گلِ یخ

اندیشهٔ شکُفتن و
گفتن حدیثِ عشق
جوشِ بهار،
درگُلِ یخ،
موج زد چنانك
-وقتی که سنگ از دمِ دی ماه می شکست-
زان پیش تر که برگ برآرد،
به گُل نشست.

Wintersweet Flower

The thought of blooming
  and recounting the love story,
The anticipation of spring
Billowed within wintersweet flower so
– as December's cold breath cracked the rock –
Before growing leaves,
It bloomed.

شیپورِ اطلسی ها

در روزگارِ عربدۀ مرگ
در غربتی که هرچه ترانه ست
از مرگ می سراید و
نومید
شیپورِ اطلسی ها
فریادِ زندگی ست
در انتظارِ رایتِ خورشید.

۵ فروردین ۱۳۸۸

98

Petunias' Trumpet

In the age of howling death
In an exile where all melodies
　　compose songs of destitution and demise
The petunias' trumpet
Is the call of life
Awaiting sunrise.

March 25, 2009

حَبَّةُ القلب

كاش می شد که روزی، دلم را
مثلِ بذری بکارم که
فردا
بارَور گردد ونسل عشّاق
از محیطِ زمین برنیفتد.
می توان ماند، ازین گونه، آیا؟

Seed of the Heart

I hope one day,
I can plant my heart like a seed
  so that
Tomorrow
It'll bear fruit and the lovers' progeny
  will not become extinct from the earth
Can one persist, in this manner, I wonder?

از بیمِ خشکسال

گُل داده ارغوانِ جوان درحیاطِ ما
در روزهای آخر اسفند
وهرچه غنچه داشته برشاخ
امروز، جمله را همگی باز کرده است

◆

او، با غریزه، دشمنِ خود را شناخته
وزبیمِ خشکسال که درراه است
یك ماه زودتر
هنگامهٔ شكفتن وگفتن را
آغازکرده است.

اسفند ۱۳۸۷

In Fear of Drought

The young Judas tree has budded in our garden
   in mid–March
And all the buds it has had on its branch,
   today, it has opened them all.

◆

It, instinctively, has identified its enemy
And in fear of the impending drought
A month earlier
It has begun
   the uproar of blooming and recounting.

February-March 2009

ساعت و تقویم

درآینه موی خویشتن را
دیدی و شدی به بیم تسلیم
وان دل که هنوز عاشق توست
بیزار زِ ساعت است و تقویم.

Clock & Calendar

You noticed your hair in the mirror and
   surrendered to fear
Yet the one who still adores you
   despises clocks & calendars.

شکوفهٔ بادام

خوشا سپیده دما
آن زمان که در اسفند
برای خوردنِ شیر از شکوفهٔ بادام
زمین به کودکیِ خویش باز می گردد.

Almond Blossom

Blessed is the March dawn
   when the earth reverts to its infancy
   to nurse on the nectar of the almond blossom.

شکُفتن

از دلِ این سنگ و از صلابتِ سرما
شاد و شکیبا و پُر شکوه شکفتن
ای گُلِ وَحشی! خدای را چه بگویم
با چه زبانی توان سپاسِ تو گفتن؟

Blooming

Sprouting out of the heart of this rock, in the
  bitter cold
  joyfully, magnificently and patiently
O wildflower! for the glory of God
What words can one use to thank you
  sufficiently?

میوهٔ مرگ

بذرِ سکوت،
ریشه دوانید و
برگ داد
وانگه هزار شاخه شد و
میوه مرگ داد.

The Fruit of Death

The seed of silence
   grew roots and
   leaves,
   a thousand branches
   and
Bore the fruit of death.

ندای هنگام

آخرین روزهای اسفند است
از سرِ شاخِ این برهنه چنار
مرغکی با ترنّمی بیدار
می زند نغمه،
نیست معلومم
آخرین شِکوه از زمستان است
یا نخستین ترانه های بهار.

The Call of the Moment

It's mid-March
On the bare branch of the plane tree
A bridling is singing
A lively melody,
It's not clear to me
Whether this is the last lamentation of
    winter
Or the first song of spring.

زیباییِ برهنگیِ باغ

آیینه ای برابرِ هر جلوه و جمال
زیباییِ برهنگیِ باغ
در روزهای آخر اسفند
آبستنی به زیورِ هر گونه احتمال.

The Beauty of the Bare Garden

A mirror of charm and luster
The beauty of the bare garden
in the last days of winter
Pregnant with possibilities.

یك دقیقه سکوت

وقتی از شاخه اوفتاد آن برگ

با چنان اضطراب و پیچاپیچ

کاروانِ کلاغ ها کردند

یك دقیقه سکوت و

دیگر هیچ.

۲۳ اردیبهشت ۱۳۷٤

A Moment of Silence

When the leaf fell to the ground
Spiraling with anguish
The caravan of crows
Observed a moment of silence
And no more.

May 13, 1995

نامِ این درخت

نامِ این درخت چیست؟
نامِ این درختِ نیك بخت چیست؟

این درختِ شاعری كه در نهایتِ خزان
آن زمان كه جمله برگ هاش ریخته ست
آن زمان كه باغ
خالی از پرنده ها و برگ هاست –
اینچنین
غرقِ گُل شده ست
مثلِ سالخورده مردمی كه ناگهان
سر به عاشقی برآورد.

نام این درخت
این درخت نیك بخت
یا كه شوربخت،
چیست؟
نامِ این درخت چیست؟

The Name of This Tree

What is the name of this tree?
What is the name of this fortunate tree?

This tree of poetry that at Fall's peak
when all its leaves have fallen to the
  ground
when the garden
is uninhabited by birds, leafless
Is thus
in full bloom

Like the elderly who suddenly
Embrace love

What is
The name of this tree
This fortunate or
unfortunate tree?
What is the name of this tree?

گویی درختِ تشنه لبی...

آبی ست آسمان و
افق باز
یك توده ابرِ كوچك،
در شیبِ درّه ها
گویی درختِ تشنه لبی
آه می كشد.

As if the Thirsty Tree....

The sky is blue and
The horizon vast
A patch of small clouds
On the valley slopes
As if the thirsty tree
Is sighing.

در چشمِ باغبان

با هر خبر که می شنوم از تو

دور،

دور،

همراه عطرِ نرگسِ قدسی

سرشار از طراوت و تکرار می شوم

چون آن نخستْ واژه که کودک

آموزد از زبان

یا اولین شکوفهٔ یك شاخ

در چشمِ باغبان.

In the Gardner's Eye

With each piece of news that I hear about you
From far,
far away,
With the heavenly scent of daffodils
I am refreshed and renewed
Like the first word
a child learns
Or the first blossom on the branch
in the gardener's eye.

چرخِ چاه

سیزیفِ ایرانی

آویخته به زمزمهٔ چرخ و ریسمان
از ژرفِ چاه، سطل به بالاست در سفر
تا می رسد به روشنیِ روز و آفتاب
وارونه می شود به بُنِ چاهِ سرد و تر.

تاریخِ سطل تجربه ای تلخ و تیره است:
تا آستانِ روشنیِ روز آمدن
پیمودن آن مسافت دشوار، با امید،
وانگه دوباره در دلِ ظلمت رها شدن.

Well Windlass

Iranian Sisyphus

Suspended from the humming of wheel and
   rope
The pale climbs up from the depths of the
   well
As it reaches daylight and sunshine
It circles back to the bottom of the cold and
   wet well

The pale's tale is a bitter and dark one
Reaching the threshold of daylight
Traveling the difficult path with hope
Yet again, released to the heart of darkness

Chronological List of Poems

What follows is the name of the collection or volume, the date and place of each poem, when indicated by the poet. The list has been organized chronologically. In cases where the poems are not dated, the date of publication of the collection or volume has been used. The natural elements present in each poem also have been listed.

WILD GARDEN
Wake Up Song, pp. 25–6, spring 1963, Mashhad.
Garden, chicory, blowball.

WHICH ANTICIPATION...?
Wake Up Song, p. 45, Jan/Feb 1964, Mashhad.
Titmouse, spring, branch.

MOUNTAIN OSIER
Wake Up Song, pp. 53–54, July/Aug 1964, Kadkan.
Mountain osier (willow), mountain, lightening, storm.

BEWARE...
Wake Up Song, pp. 73–4, Feb/March 1965, Mashhad.
Almond blossom, grove, breeze, cloud, sun, wind.

QUERY
Wake Up Song, pp. 75–6, Feb/March 1965,
 Mashhad.
Tree, breeze, branch of blossoms, spring, wind,
 cloud.

WITHSTANDING A THORN
Whispers, p. 70, 1965/66; no date (for the poem), no
 place.
Spring, fruit, leaf, branch, garden,tulip, thorn.

DOUBT
Like a Tree on a Rainy Night, pp. 50–1, Feb 1967,
 Tehran.
Spring, trees, breeze, cloud.

MIGRATION OF VIOLETS
As the Leaf Would Say, pp. 22–3, Feb/March 1967,
 no place.
Violets, spring, winter.

IN THE PRESENCE OF THE WIND
As the Leaf Would Say, pp. 50–1, July/Aug 1967, no
 place.
Stream, dawn, rain, wind.

RESPONSE
In the Back Alleys of Neyshabur, p. 70, Aug 2,1967,
 Tehran
Wave, sea.

LANGUOR
As the Leaf Would Say, pp. 63–4, Nov/Dec 1967, no
 place
Stream, water.

SEA
In the Back Alleys of Neyshabur, p. 39, 1967, Tehran
Sea, storm, swamp.

CLEAR BLUE
Like a Tree on a Rainy Night, pp. 32–3, July 5, 1968,
  Tehran.
Fir, garden.

RAIN'S TRAVELOGUE
As the Leaf Would Say, p. 17, collection published in
  1968/69, no date (for the poem), no place.
Rain, earth.

PEN AND INK
Traces of Sorrow, p. 100, 1969, Tehran.
Winter, spring, garden.

A PRAYER IN STRAIT
Like a Tree on a Rainy Night, p. 17, Jan 18, 1970,
  Tehran.
Spring, rain, tree, stream, moonlight, dawn.

YOUTH
Like a Tree on a Rainy Night, p. 47, February 12,
  1970, Tehran.
Red rose.

SAFE TRAVELS!
In the Back Alleys of Neyshabur, pp. 15–6, collection
  published in 1971/72, no date (for the poem), no
  place.
Milkvetch, desert, blossoms, rain, breeze.

POPPY'S LIFE STORY 1
Of Being and Composing, p. 57, 1971/2, Tehran.
Poppy, dawn, wind.

AUTUMNAL CLIMATE
Like a Tree on a Rainy Night, p. 60, Fall 1974, Tehran.
Chestnut tree, fall, spring.

POPPY'S LIFE STORY 2
Of Being and Composing, pp. 58–9, January 1975,
    Oxford.
Poppy, Judas tree, spring.

HYMN
Like a Tree on a Rainy Night, pp. 36–7, December 16,
    1975, Princeton.
Sunlight, spring, garden.

TREE'S PSALM
Of Being and Composing, pp. 55, December 1975,
    Oxford.
Tree, rain, thunder, blizzard.

MOURNING THE ESSENCE OF THE STORM
Traces of Sorrow, p. 106, 1975/6, no place.
Sunset, storm, thunder, spring.

JANUARY
Like a Tree on a Rainy Night, p. 53, January 1976,
    Tehran.
Pine, rain.

TOAD'S ADMONITION
In Praise of Doves, pp. 18–9, April 10, 1976, no place.
Milkvetch.

THE GREENNESS OF MOSS
Traces of Sorrow, pp. 21–2, April 17, 1976, Oxford.
Moss, river, water, rock, greenness.

WITH THE ROSE PETAL
Traces of Sorrow, p. 101, 1976, Princeton.
Raindrops, sky, fall, water, rose petal.

BEFORE THE TREE
The Scent of Moulian River, pp. 68–9, collection
    published in 1978/79, no date (for the poem), no
    place.
Spruce, robin, dawn, plant, leaflet, tree.

NO MAN'S LAND
The Scent of Moulian River, pp. 75–6, collection
    published in 1978/79, no date (for the poem), no
    place.
River, trees, birds, butterflies, swallow.

CURRENT MOOD
The Scent of Moulian River, p. 55, collection
    published in 1978-79, no date (for the poem), no
    place.
Night, dawn, morning.

INQUIRY 2
The Scent of Moulian River, p. 52, collection
    published in 1978-79, no date (for the poem), no
    place.
White jasmines, red sweetbriars (dog roses).

COLD SNAP
Traces of Sorrow, p. 61, March/April 1979, no place.
Winter, firn, dogwood winter.

SUN'S MAKEUP
An Ode to Sunflower, p. 21, Aug 14, 1987, no place.
Sun, flower, garden.

A TREELESS LEAF
An Ode to Sunflower, p. 65, Sept 3, 1987, no place.
Tree, leaf, cloud, fall, spring

LEAF OF GREEN TREES
The Comet, pp. 59–61, 1988-89, no place.
Breeze, sparrow, garden, seed, white poplar.

A JOURNEY IN THE LILY PAD
An Ode to Sunflower, pp. 71–72, 1989, no place.
Sky, spring, dawn, lily.

COMPASS★
Traces of Sorrow, pp. 80–1, April 19, 1993, no place.

CLAW TO CLAW WITH DEATH
A Child Named Joy, p. 162, April 29, 1993, no place.
Wind, leaf, branch

BLOWBALLS
Traces of Sorrow, pp. 55–6, May 15, 1993, no place.
Blowball, wind.

A MOMENT OF SILENCE
A Child Named Joy, p. 290, volume published in
    2020, May 13, 1995, no place.
Leaf, crows.

BIRD SONG
An Ode to Sunflower, p. 20, volume published in
    1997, no date (for the poem), no place.
Boxwood, bird.

SUNFLOWER
An Ode to Sunflower, p. 88, volume published in
    1997, no date (for the poem), no place.
Sunflower, sun, clouds.

FLORAL TILE DESIGN
Traces of Sorrow, p. 49, volume published in 1997, no
    date (for the poem), no place.
Sparrow, flower, spring, winter.

WELL WINDLASS★
Elegies for Kashmar's Cedar, p.38, volume published
    in 1997, no date (for the poem), no place.

IN FEAR OF DROUGHT
A Child Named Joy, p. 156, Feb/March 2009, no
    place.
Judas tree.

BLOOMING
A Child Named Joy, p. 287, March 25, 2009, no
    place.
Wildflower, winter.

PETUNIA'S TRUMPET
A Child Named Joy, p. 288, March 25, 2009, no
    place.
Petunia, sun.

POETRY THERAPY★
A Child Named Joy, p. 238, volume published in
    2020, no date (for the poem), no place.

MISSING★
A Child Named Joy, p. 39, volume published in 2020,
    no date (for the poem), no place.

In Search of that Everlasting Moment
A Child Named Joy, p. 150, volume published in
   2020, no date (for the poem), no place.
Petunia, sky.

Wintersweet Flower
A Child Named Joy, p. 312, volume published in
   2020, no date (for the poem), no place.
Wintersweet flower.

Seed of the Heart
A Child Named Joy, p. 404, volume published in
   2020, no date (for the poem), no place.
Seed, fruit.

Clock and Calendar★
A Child Named Joy, p. 370, volume published in
   2020, no date (for the poem), no place.

Almond Blossom
A Child Named Joy, p. 324, volume published in
   2020, no date (for the poem), no place.
Almond blossom, nectar.

The Fruit of Death
A Child Named Joy, p. 155, volume published in
   2020, no date (for the poem), no place.
Seed, roots, branch, fruit.

The Call of the Moment
A Child Named Joy, p. 253, volume published in
   2020, no date (for the poem), no place.
Bridling, winter, spring

★Poems with no elements of nature

Sources Used

In translating the poems contained in the first two volumes, *A Mirror for Voices* and *The Second Millennium of the Mountain Deer*, the individual collections in each volume were used. *A Mirror for Voices* includes seven collections: *Whispers, Wake Up Song, As the Leaf Would Say, In the Back Alleys of Neyshabur, Like a Tree on a Rainy Night, Of Being and Composing and the Scent of Moulian River.* *The Second Millennium of the Mountain Deer* encompasses five collections: *An Ode to Sunflower, In Praise of Doves, The Comet, Elegy for Kashmar Cedar,* and *Traces of Sorrow.* In translating the poems that appear in the most recent volume, *A Child Named Joy,* the compilation itself has been used.

COMMENTARIES ON KADKANI AND HIS POETRY

Abbassi, H., ed. *Safarnameh-ye Baran* [Rain's Travelogue] (Tehran: Sokhan, 2009).

Bashardoost, Mojtaba. *Dar Josteju-ye Neyshabur* [In Search of Neyshabur](Tehran: Saless, 2007):

Sharifi, F. *Shafi'i Kadkani*, (Tehran: Negah, 2015).

POETRY EDITIONS

Shafi'i Kadkani, M.R., *Zemzemeha* [Whispers] (Tehran: Sokhan, 2009): 70.

———. *Shabkhuni* [Wake Up Song] (Tehran: Sokhan, 2009): 25, 26, 45, 53, 54, 73, 74, 75, 76.

———. (2009). *Az Zaban-e Barg* [As the Leaf Would Say] (Tehran: Sokhan, 2009): 17, 22, 23, 50, 51,63, 64.

———. *Dar Koocheh Baghha-ye Neyshabur* [In the Back Alleys of Neyshabur] (Tehran: Sokhan, 2009): 15, 16, 39, 70.

———. *Mesl-e Derakht dar Shab-e Baran* [Like a Tree on a Rainy Night] (Tehran: Sokhan, 2009): 17, 32, 33, 36, 37, 47, 50, 51, 53, 60.

———. *Az Boodan-o Sorudan* [Of Being and Composing]. (Tehran: Sokhan, 2009): 55, 57, 58, 59.

———. *Boo-ye Ju-ye Muliyan* [The Scent of Muliyan River] (Tehran: Sokhan, 2009): 52,55, 68, 69, 75, 76.

———. *Khati ze Deltangi* [Traces of Sorrow]. (Tehran: Sokhan, 2009): 21, 22, 49, 55, 56, 61, 80, 81, 100, 101, 106.

———. *Ghazali Bara-ye Gol-e Aftabgarda*n [An Ode to Sunflower] (Tehran: Sokhan, 2009): 20, 21, 65, 71,72, 88.

———. *Setareh Donbalehdar* [The Comet] (Tehran: Sokhan, 2009): 59, 60, 61.

———. *Dar Setayesh-e Kabutarha* [In Praise of Doves](Tehran: Sokhan, 2009): 18, 19.

———. *Marsieh-ha-ye Sarv-e Kashmar* [Elegies for Kashmar Cedar] (Tehran: Sokhan, 2009): 38.

Acknowledgments

I initially started this project to share a single poem with my daughter, Tina, and then went on to translate the second poem and the third and. . . . She has been my cheerleader, my first reader, the most caring critic and editor as well as my inspiration.

I would like to thank Shaz Serene for the cover paintings; Karen Odden, Sue Ano, Sayeh Eghtesadinia, Debbie Rusch, Arjang Assad and Hadi Bahar for helping me find the most precise words at all hours, and for their love and encouragement.

Other Mage Poetry Titles

Song of the Ground Jay: Poems by Iranian Women, 1960–2022
Bilingual Edition / Selected and Translated by Mojdeh Bahar

Faces of Love: Hafez and the Poets of Shiraz
Bilingual Edition / Translated by Dick Davis

The Mirror of My Heart:
A Thousand Years of Persian Poetry by Women
Bilingual Edition / Translated by Dick Davis

Vis and Ramin
Fakhraddin Gorgani / Translated by Dick Davis

Khosrow and Shirin
Nezami Ganjavi / Translated by Dick Davis

Layli and Majnun
Nezami Ganjavi / Translated by Dick Davis

Shahnameh: The Persian Book of Kings
Abolqasem Ferdowsi / Translated by Dick Davis

Rostam: Tales of Love and War from Persia's Book of Kings
Abolqasem Ferdowsi / Translated by Dick Davis

Borrowed Ware: Medieval Persian Epigrams
Introduced and Translated by Dick Davis

When They Broke Down the Door: Poems
Fatemeh Shams / Introduction and translations by Dick Davis

Another Birth and Other Poems
By Forugh Farrokhzad, translated by Hasan Javadi
and Susan Sallée / Bilingual edition

Obeyd-e Zakani: Ethics of Aristocrats and other Satirical Works
translated by Hasan Javadi

Audio Books

Faces of Love: Hafez and the Poets of Shiraz
Translated by Dick Davis / Penguin Audio / Read by
Dick Davis, Tala Ashe and Ramiz Monsef

The Mirror of My Heart:
A Thousand Years of Persian Poetry by Women
Translated by Dick Davis / Penguin Audio / Read by
Dick Davis, Mozhan Marno, Tala Ashe and Serena Manteghi

Layli and Majnun
Nezami Ganjavi / Translated by Dick Davis
Penguin Audio / Read by
Dick Davis, Peter Ganim, Serena Manteghi and Sean Rohani

Vis and Ramin
Fakhraddin Gorgani / Translated by Dick Davis
Mage Audio / Read by
Mary Sarah Agliotta, Dick Davis (introduction)

My Uncle Napoleon
Iraj Pezeshkzad / Translated by Dick Davis
Mage Audio / Read by
Moti Margolin, Dick Davis (introduction)

Savushun: A Novel about Modern Iran
Simin Daneshvar / Translated by M.R. Ghanoonparvar
Mage Audio / Read by
Mary Sarah Agliotta, Brian Spooner (introduction)

Crowning Anguish: Taj al-Saltana
Memoirs of a Persian Princess
from the Harem to Modernity, 1884–1914
Introduction by Abbas Amanat / Translated by Anna Vanzan
Mage Audio / Read by
Kathreen Khavari

www.ingramcontent.com/pod-product-compliance
Lightning Source LLC
Chambersburg PA
CBHW030457100426
42813CB00002B/250